HOCKEY CANADA

The SPECTACULAR SIDNEY CROSBY

ANDREW PODNIEKS

FENN

Fenn Publishing Company Ltd.
Bolton, Canada

Fenn Publishing Company Ltd.

THE SPECTACULAR SIDNEY CROSBY

A Fenn Publishing Book / First Published in 2005

Designed by First Image

Fenn Publishing Company Ltd.
Bolton, Ontario, Canada

Printed in Canada

Library and Archives Canada Cataloguing in Publication
Podnieks, Andrew
The spectacular Sidney Crosby / Andrew Podnieks.
ISBN 1-55168-304-0

1. Crosby, Sidney, 1987-   2. Hockey players--Canada--Biography.   I. Title.
GV848.5.C76P63 2005   796.962'092   C2005-904634-1

Cover photo: Dave Sandford-Hockey Canada/Hockey Hall of Fame (Team Canada)
and Reuters (Pittsburgh)

CONTENTS

Sidney pauses after winning silver at the 2004 World Junior Championship in Finland.

PRELUDE

When 16-year-old Sydney Crosby attended Team Canada's final selection camp to prepare for the 2004 World Junior Championship in Helsinki, Finland, the coaching staff roomed him with Jeff Tambellini, a 19-year-old from Calgary playing hockey that season for the University of Michigan Wolverines. Sidney, from tiny Cole Harbour, Nova Scotia, was among the youngest players ever to play in the tournament.

Jeff was the son of Steve Tambellini who had been in a similar position some 25 years earlier at the 1978 World Junior tournament. At that time, Steve was roomed with a skinny little 16-year-old kid named Wayne Gretzky, and Jeff knew very well that the comparisons between himself and his father—and the Great One and Sidney – were intentional. "I talked to my dad about it," Jeff agreed, "and he said that even though he [Gretzky] was a great talent back then, he was nervous and just happy to be included in a group of good players." Jeff then related his dad's words to his own experience. "Sidney was the same way. He was nervous and excited. I just tried to get him to relax."

> Sidney was among the youngest players ever to play in the tournament.

BOY WONDER

CHAPTER ONE

Sidney was a star at the Air Canada Cup with his team from Nova Scotia.

"That's all Sidney would want to do—play hockey."

Trina Crosby, Sidney's mom

Cole Harbour, Nova Scotia is a small, quiet, and pretty town on Route 207 about halfway between Halifax and the Atlantic Ocean. There isn't a lot to do in Cole Harbour. When Sidney Crosby was growing up there, he liked to do one thing more than anything else—play hockey.

"When he was three or four," his mother, Trina, told, "I bought him a toy gas station. He didn't play with that thing once. He would rather do something where he was competing. He always had a ton of energy."

Trina laughed. "I used to pick him up from daycare when he was three and this little old lady would bring him to me and she'd say, 'I can't play hockey with him every day.' That's all Sidney would want to do—play hockey. He couldn't get enough of it."

On a lot of days, Sidney would go downstairs to the family basement where he set up a sheet of Plexiglas on the floor between the family's washing machine and dryer to practice his shooting. When his shot got so hard that the puck bounced off the wall and hit him, he started shooting through the doorway. "There were a lot of marks on the door," Sidney admitted with a smile. "I also had my grandmother sit in a chair in the family room. She wasn't very old, and she played goalie and could move pretty well. I'd shoot on her, too."

At nights, Sidney loved to watch television where he could admire his NHL heroes play—Wayne Gretzky, Steve Yzerman, Mario Lemieux. "Sidney has always had good role models," his father, Troy, said, referring to those NHL superstars who were both tremendous players on the ice and ambassadors for the game off it. "He sees how they can be great hockey players as well as great people," Troy explained.

> *When Sidney Crosby was growing up, he liked to do one thing more than anything else— play hockey*

As a kid, Sidney tried always to wear number nine, the number worn by many great stars of the past.

Sidney first started skating when he was three years old but he wasn't allowed to play organized hockey until he was five. Right from the very start, though, he played against older kids and was still always the best player on the ice. His first team was the Dartmouth Timbits, and even then his father could see that his son was special. "He seemed to pick up hockey easily," Troy explained. "The skills of it – shooting, passing, skating – came easily to him, even at five. You could tell he was advancing faster than other kids his age."

In 1994, when he was seven years old, Sidney impressed a much older local boy named Brad Richards. Brad was 14 at that time. In the summer he helped out at select hockey camps in Halifax, not far from his home in Murray Harbour, Prince Edward Island. "You could see, even then, [Sidney] was so much better than anyone else on the ice," Brad recalled. "He would go up against guys who were two, three years older than him and dominate." From those first days forward, Brad was a role model of sorts for Sidney.

What impressed Brad as much as the young boy's skill was how Sidney behaved away from the rink. Sidney stayed away from drinking pop or any other bad drinks with sugar in them. He drank only bottled water. Brad knows what he's talking about and his opinion should be respected. He made it to the NHL in the year 2000 and just four years later he led the Tampa Bay Lightning to an amazing Stanley Cup win. Brad was also named Conn Smythe Trophy winner that year as most valuable player in the playoffs. He deserved the honour. After all, Tampa Bay won 16 playoff games that year, and Brad scored seven, game-winning goals! That was an all-time, NHL record.

> "The skills of it – shooting, passing, skating – came easily to him, even at five. You could tell he was advancing faster than other kids his age."

Sidney watches the linesman's hand in preparation for a faceoff during the Air Canada Cup.

Although he was a gifted hockey player, Sidney was still just a young boy and had a long way to go in developing as a person as well as athlete before anyone was going to call him spectacular. One day, Sidney learned an important hockey lesson from his dad. "We were driving home from a game," Trina explained, "and Sidney started complaining about a mistake a defenceman had made. Troy turned to him and asked, 'Do you think you were perfect today?' Sidney said no. Troy told him just to worry about himself and never mind what others do. Sidney got the message."

Sidney's Dartmouth Subways team went farther in the tournament than any other team from the province ever had before.

By the time Sidney was ten years old, he was already doing amazing things on the ice. He played atom in Cole Harbour and recorded 159 goals and 280 total points in just 55 games, an average of more than five points per game over the course of a whole season! Of course, this still didn't come close to Gretzky who, at the same age, scored an unbelievable 378 goals in 85 games at age ten!

It was when he was 14 years old, during the 2001-02 hockey season, that people from all over Canada started to hear stories about this incredible young hockey player from Nova Scotia. Sidney played that year for the Dartmouth Subways Midget AAA team in a league where most of the players were two or three years older than him. Still, Sidney led the league in scoring with 193 points in 74 games. He also led the team to the finals of the Air Canada Cup, the national championship for that age group. It was the first time a team from the Maritimes had made it that far.

"He has the ability to raise his game to another level and has an innate understanding of what's going to happen a play ahead of everyone else."

The Dartmouth Subways got to the finals of that tournament when Sidney scored at 19:28 of the third period of the semifinals to give his team an historic place in the championship game. "I always want the puck when the game's on the line," he said later. "I love that challenge, especially when the games are big. I just want my team to win so badly that I'd do anything." The tournament, held in Bathurst, New Brunswick, saw Sidney lead the points standings. He was also made tournament MVP, the youngest player ever so honoured.

Sidney's coach with the Subways, Brad Crossley, was very impressed by how the young boy played, but he was not surprised. "He's a revelation to everyone else," Brad said after the Air Canada Cup, "but he's fitting in just the way I expected him to.

He has the ability to raise his game to another level and he has an innate understanding of what's going to happen a play ahead of everyone else. He's head and shoulders above everyone on the ice."

Sidney's special connection to hockey is very simple. He loves the game, and he has a great desire to improve every day. For instance, one day during his midget year with Dartmouth, school in Cole Harbour was cancelled because of a bad snowstorm. Sidney went to the Dartmouth Sportsplex to see if he and some friends could play shinny. It was early morning, and the arena manager said okay. Over the next several hours friends joined in the game, played for a while, and left, exhausted. By dinner hour, only Sidney remained. "That's an example of the kind of thing he does," Troy said. "His friends were there for a couple of hours and they took off, but most of the time it was just him, working with the puck, doing drills, having fun."

Fun? How's this for fun? That summer, the summer of 2002, Sidney got his first taste of true hockey glory. He was invited to Los Angeles, California, to play in a 3-on-3 hockey game with the Great One himself, Wayne Gretzky. The camp was hosted by a player-agent company called IMG (International Management Group). It was intended for 18- and 19-year-old players who were hoping to play in the NHL soon. Sidney, at 14 years of age, was a special guest. "I just had to get on the ice with him," Wayne said of his first encounter with Sidney. "He has everything.

Sidney makes a move by sliding the puck through an opponent's skates and then chasing after it.

People say Canadians don't have enough finesse, but he sure does. He has a love for the game. He does the right things. He's a good kid. More importantly at his age, he has good guidance from his parents."

Like Brad Richards, Wayne saw in this young star not just the hockey skills but the character to support those skills. "The thing I like most about him is that he loves hockey," the Great One said. "He is on the ice all day long, and he loves to play. He is as good as anyone I have seen in a long time."

And Sidney's response to playing with #99, the NHL's all-time leading scorer? "It's not too hard to play with him," he said, smiling. "All you have to do is keep your stick on the ice."

Troy Crosby knew how special the trip was for his son. "It was a great learning experience. He learned a lot from guys like Jason Spezza and Pierre-Marc Bouchard. He learned how to prepare properly and how to handle himself off the ice."

That short training session with Wayne Gretzky proved to be the start of a great summer for Sidney. Stan Butler, a former junior coach with Canada's national team, was at the camp in California teaching the players. He was so impressed by Sidney that he called Marc Habscheid, the coach of Team Canada for the 2003 World Junior Championship which was going to take place in Halifax.

Stan suggested that Sidney be invited to the national summer camp in that city so that the youngster could experience the process of the world juniors for the following year when everyone hoped he would play on the team. Just being around the best players under 20 years of age and learning from them was reason enough for Sidney to accept the invitation.

Sidney drew interest from fans and scouts right across the country for his play at the Air Canada Cup.

So, just after Sidney's 15th birthday, there he was with the best junior players in all of Canada, working as stick boy, towel boy, and water boy, learning and seeing how a national camp operated. He didn't skate with the team, but coach Habscheid made him feel like a player, inviting him to stay in the dorms with the juniors and taking part in all of the team activities.

Over the course of the summer, Sidney also had to make a huge decision about where to go to school. He talked to his parents, and together they decided it would be best for him to go to Minnesota to play what was called "prep school hockey." This was a serious level of hockey in the United States at a high school where both studies and pucks were important. It was also a place where Sidney could be just Sidney—no reporters, no pressure from other parents watching him play.

Sidney's hockey future looked amazingly bright. He had all the skills, talent, and determination to become a superstar in the NHL one day. But his parents realized that he needed a level-headed plan at this stage of his life. He was only 15 years old. If he were injured today and couldn't play any more, his education would be critical to his success in the world. No one was more aware of this than his father, Troy, who started on a hockey career along with another goalie, the great Patrick Roy.

Sidney recalled the first time he watched Patrick and the Montreal Canadiens play. "I was around five or six when they [the Canadiens] won the Cup [in 1993]," he said. "It was kind of the first time I could actually understand what was going on. They had guys like Patrick Roy and John LeClair." In 1984, the Montreal Canadiens drafted two goalies. They chose Patrick Roy, of course, and he went on to have a spectacular, Hall of Fame career. They also chose Troy Crosby.

Troy went on to win the Quebec league championship in 1985 with another future NHL star, Claude Lemieux, in Verdun, but Troy never had any greater success. By the time he was 19, his days of playing serious hockey were pretty much over. "It left me with not much of an opportunity to further my education," he reflected, sadly.

With this in mind, Troy would never let Sidney give up his education simply because he was a good hockey player. "He's a lot better in school than I was at that age [15]," Troy admitted. "He's a little more mature and he knows the importance of education. I just know from experience. Everyone thinks they're going to make it to the NHL, but so few do. It's important to have an education."

Troy is not the only near-family member to influence Sidney's love of hockey. His uncle, Robby Forbes, was a legend in senior hockey in Newfoundland who also played overseas in Great Britain and The Netherlands. One cousin, Forbes MacPherson, has played professional hockey in the minor leagues for years. Another cousin, Robby Sutherland, was captain of the Halifax Mooseheads in the Quebec league. A third cousin, Jeff Sutherland, played at Dalhousie University in Halifax. All were great hockey players, which was impressive, but none made the NHL, which showed Sidney that nothing in life was a sure thing.

THE SPECTACULAR ✦ SIDNEY CROSBY

No one was more aware of this than his father, Troy, who started on a hockey career along with another goalie, the great Patrick Roy.

A YEAR IN MINNESOTA

Sidney wearing the home (far right) and road (above) sweaters of his high-school team at Shattuck-St. Mary's in Minnesota.

"He's a really nice boy... and a great teammate."

Tom Ward, St. Mary's coach

The name of the school that Sidney decided to go to was Shattuck-St. Mary's, located in Faribault, Minnesota. That school's hockey program was operated by J.P. Parise, one of Canada's players on the 1972 Summit Series team, perhaps the greatest team of all time. J.P.'s own son, Zach, also played on the team. Zach, though, like almost everyone else on the team, was two years older than Sidney. J.P. could see right away that Sidney was special because he was as good a player but much younger.

Even though the school was quite small (just 300 students), Sidney had a difficult time adjusting. He was an incredible hockey player, for sure, but he was still a 15-year-old boy living on his own far away from home. "It was lonely," he admitted. "At the start it was really hard. I would find myself crying when I woke up in the morning because it was such a different world. It wasn't until classes started up and the hockey season began that I felt comfortable because the day was so full by then and at the end of the night you were too exhausted to think about it."

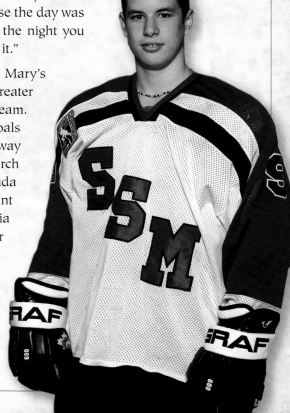

Sidney spent his year at St. Mary's developing his hockey skills at a greater rate than everyone else on the team. He set a league record with 72 goals and 162 points in 57 games. Midway through the year (February 22-March 1, 2003), he returned home to Canada to take part in another important event. He played for the Nova Scotia hockey team at the Canada Winter Games. This had been part of his plan all along. When he first got to Shattuck, he requested these days off especially to be able to play in the tournament.

Captain Sidney led a provincial team from Nova Scotia at the Canada Winter Games in February 2003.

"It's going to be fun to see some of my old teammates and just to be back in Bathurst [New Brunswick], where I had probably the best hockey experience I've had up to this point," he said, referring to the previous year's historic silver medal with the Dartmouth Subways at the Air Canada Cup. "The last time I had a lot of pressure, I came through, so I'm going to look at it the same way. I'm not going to try to change anything. I'll play hockey the way I know how to play." Sidney did just that. Again, he was voted the best player in the whole tournament.

It was also at the Canada Winter Games that Sidney started wearing the famous number 87 on his sweater. He had a very good reason—two good reasons, actually—for choosing this seemingly strange number. First, Sidney was born on August 7 (the eighth month and the seventh day). Second, he was born in the year 1987. Thus, he took 87.

The Spectacular Sidney Crosby

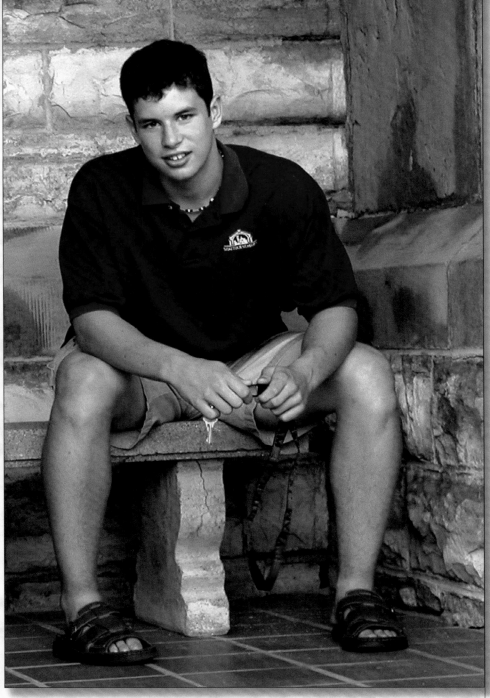

Off ice, Sidney was just another student at Shattuck.

Upon returning to school in Minnesota, Sidney played so well that the team qualified to play in the USA Hockey Tier I tournament. This was the most important event in the United States for players under 17 years of age. Sidney's team, St. Mary's, beat Illinois 5-4 in the finals to win the championship.

No one was more impressed with Sidney than his coach at St. Mary's, Tom Ward. "The first time I saw him was a year ago (2002) at the Mac's midget tournament in Calgary when he was playing for the Dartmouth Subways," Tom began. "He looked then like a very skilled 14-year-old playing up a level. He was smart, had the puck a whole lot and made good plays, but he wasn't quite as big and strong as the other boys. The Sidney who came to school this year was older and stronger. He's got strong legs and great balance," Tom marveled.

Later, he described Sidney's skills in greater detail: "He's not a huge guy, but he's strong for his size and he's got great puck-protection skills. He's got great vision and he's skilful with the puck. He moves it very well and he shares it very well. And he's a really nice boy and is a great teammate. He's now learning how to play from goal line to goal line. He wants that responsibility, and he's not just a one-dimensional player. He wants to be a complete player, and he's also learning to take on some leadership on our team."

Sidney fights off a check during his record-breaking season with Shattuck.

Sidney was not just a great hockey player; he had a great attitude to life which he brought to the rink and to the world around him. "He's a team-oriented kid," his coach explained. "Sidney has had a lot of adulation, and he's been able to keep his feet on the ground. He works every day in practice to improve his game. He's a good friend to his friends in school away from the rink."

By season's end, Sidney and his parents knew that although it was tough being apart, it was an important step in life. "It was good for him," Trina admitted. "He developed as a hockey player and as a human being."

That summer, the summer of 2003, Sidney had plenty more excitement in his life. He was selected first overall by Rimouski Oceanic in the Quebec Major Junior Hockey League draft. That meant he now had to decide whether to play major junior hockey in Canada to prepare for the NHL or return to St. Mary's for another season of high–school hockey in Minnesota before continuing at an American college. "He's already heard from about ten schools," his father admitted, discussing the college option, "including Michigan, Wisconsin, North Dakota, and Minnesota. He can pretty well go to any school he wants in the US." Rimouski, on the other hand, was a small town in Quebec with a population of about 50,000. It was located on the south bank of the St. Lawrence River and was a lot more like Cole Harbour.

What did Sidney do? He called his friend Brad Richards, now a star in the NHL. Sidney remembered that Brad had played with Rimouski for three years. In fact, Brad's number 39 sweater hangs in the rafters of the Rimouski arena because of his success with the Oceanic. The two had stayed in touch and followed each other's careers because Brad often served as referee or instructor at various camps Sidney had attended over the years. And, of course, Sidney followed the NHL very closely. He knew all about Brad's team, the Tampa Bay Lightning, and Brad's incredible rise as one of the league's best young players.

"He wanted to know about the school [in Rimouski]," Brad said about their conversation. "He wanted to know about the classes, how good the school was, if there was a commitment to education with the team." After getting all the answers, Sidney decided to play in Canada, in Rimouski, a small, hockey-mad city that would welcome him with open arms. The level of hockey was going to be much higher than high school in Minnesota, but that's exactly the challenge Sidney wanted and needed.

THE SPECTACULAR SIDNEY CROSBY

Sidney was not just a great hockey player; he had a great attitude to life which he brought to the rink and to the world around him.

SIDNEY JOINS RIMOUSKI

CHAPTER THREE

Bigger, stronger, and more mature, Sidney joined the Quebec major junior league at 16 years of age.

"He's dynamite."

Wayne Gretzky

The summer of 2003 also saw young Sidney make history in another way. He was invited to the Team Canada training camp for the Under-18 Junior World Cup, an important tournament that was being held in the Czech Republic late in the summer. This was the first time Hockey Canada had ever invited a16-year-old to that tournament, but the scouting staff felt that Sidney was so good they had to make an exception. It's a good thing they did. He made the team, led the team in scoring, and helped Canada finish in fourth place that year.

It was at about this time that an interview Wayne Gretzky had given to a little-known newspaper in Phoenix called *The Arizona Republic* became the talk of the hockey world. In it, number 99 praised Sidney as the next great superstar of the NHL, a player so good he could break some of the dozens of records the Great One himself held. "He's dynamite," Wayne told the reporter. Sidney was stunned when he heard of Wayne's high praise, but he responded humbly. "I realize there will not be another Gretzky, and I will be the first one to say I will not break his records. But for him to say that I could means I'm doing something right. It was probably the best compliment I could get. I'm going to remember it for a long time."

With these words of support in his heart, it was on to major junior hockey for Sidney. The junior level was the most important stepping–stone to the NHL. As a result, Sidney looked forward to his rookie season with both pleasure and anxiety, knowing this was to be the biggest test of his life. "It's serious hockey," he said. "A lot of people from this league are going to go on and play professional hockey."

As it turned out, Sidney had little to worry about. In four pre-season games with Rimouski, Sidney recorded 14 points and was the team's most productive player. In the season opener, in a small town called Rouyn-Noranda, his Oceanic team was trailing 3-1 in the third period when he took control. He scored three successive goals—a natural hat trick!—and the Oceanic won the game, 4-3. He was named the game's first star.

In Rimouski's home opener a few nights later, Sidney had five points and led the team to victory over Moncton. He had an assist on the game-tying goal in the final minute of regulation time, and then he scored the game winner himself just nine seconds into overtime!

Almost instantly he became the league's leading scorer, and he remained at the top of the points standings until the end of the season. "Crosbymania" had arrived in Quebec, and it spread like wildfire. Everywhere he went, arenas were packed to see the sensational 16-year-old. One team would attract a crowd of 3,000 fans on a typical night, but the next night Sidney and the Oceanic would draw 10,000 fans to the same building!

And then came 'The Goal.' On November 28, 2003, during an easy 7-1 win by Rimouski over the Quebec Remparts, Sidney tried a fancy move. Standing behind the Remparts' net, he flipped the puck onto the blade of his stick, lacrosse-style, and then wrapped his stick behind the goalie from behind the goal and simply put the puck in the net while it was still flat on the blade of his stick! He was so happy that this trick move worked that he celebrated the amazing goal as if he had won the Stanley Cup. This made Don Cherry upset, and on the next episode of Coach's Corner on *Hockey Night in Canada* he said, "I like the kid." He then added, "This is a hot dog move...He can't be a hot dog like that."

From the moment he played his first game of junior, Sidney was the most dominant teenager in all of Canada.

Sidney makes a move on goalie Marc-Andre Fleury of Cape Breton in Quebec league action during the '03–'04 season.

Although a goal scorer and fancy puckhandler, Sidney could also play rough in front of the net when he had to.

Sidney saw things differently. "I worked on a move that I tried for the first time in a game and it worked. That was basically the point behind it. It wasn't to taunt or to show off...I thought I'd give it a try and it worked, so I was happy." His friend, Brad Richards, defended the trick play. "I know he's not that kind of kid," Brad said. "He's out there having fun."

In December 2003, more than 14,000 people jammed into the Colisée in Quebec City to see Sidney play. That was more than double the number of fans that showed up for a game a few nights earlier featuring another team, a Sidney-less team. Whenever he played in Halifax, not far from his home in Cole Harbour, a packed house of 10,595 always turned up to cheer him.

Sidney firing a puck from a bad angle.

The scoring, the comments by the Great Gretzky, the entertainment and excitement, all made Sidney the most popular player in the league. And every day, he tried to improve his French to get along better with the people of Rimouski.

"Every night, I want to be a better player," Sidney recited, like a creed. "If I improve, I can keep going." He even managed to impress the recently-retired Patrick Roy who was now an owner of the Quebec Remparts. "He is explosive," Patrick agreed. He then listed the things that impressed him the most. "Very fast on his skates. Controls the puck very well. Exciting to watch." But the great goalie was also more cautious in predicting Sidney's future. "Sidney is a very good junior player," Patrick admitted. "I'm sure he's going to make the NHL one day, but at what level? Time will tell."

CANADA CALLING

Sidney's goal here against Daniel Manzato of Switzerland made him the youngest player ever to score at the World Junior Championship.

"I've accomplished a lot for being 16."

Sidney Crosby

In December 2003, midway through his first year with Rimouski, Sidney got the one phone call he had been waiting for all year long. He was invited to Canada's national junior camp—not as water boy or stick boy like the previous year, but as a player! Just like in the summer with the under-18 team, Hockey Canada had decided Sidney was also among the best players in the country under the age of 20. Sure, he was only 16, and almost any other 16-year-old never would have received an invitation. But at the time he got the call, Sidney was the leading scorer in junior hockey in all of Canada with 33 goals and 76 points in 33 games. How could Hockey Canada not invite him?

Hockey Canada head scout Blair Mackasey made clear that he expected Sidney to contribute to the team. "Sidney can generate a lot of excitement, make things happen with the puck, and that is what we expect him to do. We didn't bring him in to be a defensive specialist."

Sidney was also among the best players in the country under the age of 20.

"What impresses me is the speed he carries through the neutral zone," Blair explained. "He's very competitive and plays with a lot of bite. He's physically stronger than a lot of people think. Actually, he does everything well," he said, and went on to explain. "He's not just a finesse player because he's more competitive than that. You can't call him just a speed guy, either, because he thinks so well. Defensively, he's also very good."

It was a dream come true. Yes, Sidney had worn the red and white of Canada's national team before, at the under-18 tournament. But this was junior hockey at its best, the highest level a player can play before becoming a professional. Sidney had hoped for the phone call, dreamed of the phone call, but until it came he never believed it would happen. Still, the invitation alone was not his real goal. "Any time you can play for Team Canada, it's unbelievable," he said. "It's good to be invited, but the job's not done until you're on the team."

The World Junior Championship was played every year starting on December 25 or 26 and going until the first week of the new year. When Sidney was a little kid, he didn't care about Christmas presents so much as watching that tournament. "After the presents were opened," Troy said, "Sidney would turn on the television to watch the world juniors."

Now, with that one phone call, he just might be playing in the tournament!

Sidney knew what kind of a player he was and knew he could contribute to the team. "I like initiating the play...I want to play my hardest...I love battling and making things happen," he said during camp when someone asked him to describe his style of play. It must have worked because on the last day of camp, Sidney's name was on the final roster for Finland! "To be here on the final morning [of training camp] and make it with the rest of the guys is pretty amazing," he said with a broad smile that only a 16-year-old winner can make.

Sidney Crosby was now a member of Team Canada, and that was all that mattered to him. "I want to score goals and make things happen," he said, "but I will accept any role given to me in order to help this team win." It was this kind of positive attitude that got him a little bit further every day he played hockey.

A small but true show of Sidney's skills came one day just before Christmas when the players were having some fun after practice. Sidney challenged the Team Canada goalie, Marc-Andre Fleury, to a showdown contest, best two of three penalty shots. This wasn't just any game, though. Marc-Andre had won a silver medal with Canada the year before at the World

Sidney battles a Swiss player during the same game he scored his first goal for Canada.

Sidney's family celebrates Christmas in 2003—mom (Trina), sister (Taylor), and dad (Troy).

Juniors—the year Sidney was water boy—and this season Marc-Andre was playing in the NHL, with the Pittsburgh Penguins. Sidney scored twice and was stopped only once, giving further proof that the 16-year-old could actually score on an NHL-quality goaltender!

Sidney became just the fifth 16-year-old to make Canada's junior team. Each of the other four players have all turned out to be spectacular NHL players—Wayne Gretzky, Eric Lindros, Jason Spezza, and Jay Bouwmeester. What was just as special was that when he went to Finland with the team, his parents also came. They brought with them a banner signed by hundreds of Cole Harbour residents wishing Sidney good luck at the tournament.

Sidney was 16 years old playing with the best 19-year-olds in the world. That meant that for the first time in his life, he wasn't going to be the best player during these two weeks. He did what the coaches asked of him. He played hard when given the chance. And, he watched and learned. The coaches knew they were preparing him for next year as much as giving him a chance this year.

> *He played hard when given the chance.*

In the team's first game, a hard-fought 3-0 win over hometown Finland on Boxing Day, Sidney didn't play very much, but when he did he looked good. In his next game, he made history.

Sidney became the youngest player ever in the World Junior Championships to score. He beat goalie Daniel Manzato of Switzerland with a high shot after breezing by defenceman Florian Blatter in the final minute of an easy 7-2 win for Team Canada. Again, Sidney didn't get very much ice time, but he made the most of his chances.

After a lop-sided 10-0 win over the Ukraine in which Sidney scored another goal, Canada faced the Czechs. It was the final round-robin game before the playoff elimination games began.

Sidney started the team to victory in the first period when he made an amazing play to create Canada's first goal. First, he forced a turnover in the Czech end. Then, he raced to the corner to get the loose puck. Finally, he put a perfect pass between two defencemen onto Jeff Tambellini's stick in the slot. Jeff simply redirected the pass into the net, and Canada had the early, and critical, 1-0 lead.

Canada went on to score twice more in the period and won the game 5-2, thanks in large part to the first goal created by Sidney. Jeff had nothing but praise for his roommate afterwards—except for one major problem: "He just listens to too much music," Jeff said of Sidney with a big smile. "I have to get him to turn off Shania Twain every night."

Sidney fights off a check to get a great scoring chance in the gold-medal game against USA.

Sidney was having the time of his life in Finland with Team Canada. He was making a contribution on the ice, and off it his teammates accepted him as a talented player and young friend. Canada faced the Czechs again in the semi-finals, and this time the score was an even more-lopsided 7-1 count for Canada as the team advanced to the finals for the third straight year. Canada's record was now a perfect 5-0-0.

Team Canada went on to win a silver medal after losing 4-3 to his friend Zach Parise and the USA in the gold-medal game, but everyone knew there would be more gold for Sidney in the future. He played well and showed amazing passing ability. Most important, the team was better with him in the lineup. The heart-breaking loss, though, only fuelled Sidney's ambitions for the future. "Ever since the game ended," he said after arriving in Canada from Finland after the gold medal loss,

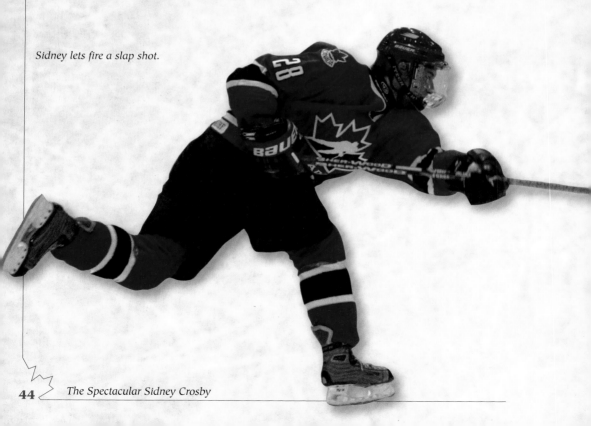

Sidney lets fire a slap shot.

The Spectacular Sidney Crosby

"[next year] is all I've been thinking about. That feeling you have after losing is not fun. You want to make sure you don't have that again."

Before leaving Rimouski to join the junior camp, Sidney was leading the Quebec league in scoring. When he returned to play, after missing a month, he was still the leading scorer! By the end of the season, he won six individual trophies at the QMJHL's awards ceremonies: the Jean Béliveau Trophy as the league's leading scorer (54 goals and 81 assists for 135 points in just 59 games); Most Valuable Player; Rookie of the Year; Offensive Player of the Year; Offensive Rookie of the Year; and, Personality of the Year. He also won the Canada Post Cup for most points earned for Three Star selections. Not bad for a 16-year-old who, at 5'10" and 185 pounds, played a season against men three years older and 25 pounds heavier. "I didn't expect to adjust so fast," he admitted. "I seemed to be able to step right in there the first game and feel comfortable. I know it's going to be tougher next year. I'm not going to surprise anyone."

Every scout who watched Sidney play believed that he would be selected first overall at the 2005 NHL Entry Draft. No one else was as skilled as he was for his age group. "That's a long way away," Sidney said about the draft, still two years in the future. "That [NHL] draft isn't just one region for junior or something like that. That's the whole world. That means I'd have to be the best player in the world for my age to go Number One and that's something that would definitely be a dream. I have so much work to do before I can even think about something like that."

Every hockey expert who watched Sidney play had something amazing to say about him. "Great speed," said one scout. "Excellent passer," said another. "Pure goal scorer." "Reliable in his own end." "Most competitive player around." "Loves to play." "Mean and nasty." "Colourful and entertaining—

> **"But I still haven't played one game in the NHL. That's my dream."**

worth the price of admission." "Mature on ice and off." "Hard worker." "Unselfish with the puck." "Improves at every level he plays."

No wonder Wayne Gretzky liked him!

Most of all, though, Sidney Crosby was able to remain level-headed and humble. When he's at home, he and his younger sister, eight-year-old Taylor, are equal, and like any brother and sister, they fight every now and then as well. Sidney also has to do his share of the housework. He has to empty the dishwasher, cut the grass, and take out the garbage. "We taught him to be a good person and treat others like he wanted to be treated," Trina explained. "He's sensitive to other people. He's thoughtful."

The family basement is testament to his on-ice accomplishments. It has pucks and medals and sweaters, a copy of the first interview he had, at age seven, covers from *The Hockey News* and a recent profile that appeared in *Sports Illustrated*. And then there is the silver medal from the World Junior Championship. "He doesn't like that one much," his father said, meaning that gold is the colour of Sidney's dreams.

When he's in Rimouski playing hockey, he talks to his parents every day, and he knows that all of his success in the past does not guarantee anything for the future. He also knows that he's blessed with a special talent and that he's living the dream of every Canadian boy. Even if he doesn't make it to the NHL, he's done more than most 16-year-olds will ever do in hockey.

"I've accomplished a lot for being 16," he said with pride, "and I'm happy with that. But I still haven't played one game in the NHL. That's my dream. That's what I'm working toward. I have a long way to go."

For his rookie season with Rimouski, Sidney earned many honours the night of his first awards ceremony in the spring of 2004.

BECOMING A WORLD CHAMPION

A bigger and faster Sidney became a leader for Canada at the 2005 World Junior Championship, a golden tournament for the team and country.

"It's pretty easy to play with Sidney. He's just got such great vision."

Patrice Bergeron

As Sidney prepared for his second season in major junior hockey with Rimouski, he knew he would have to work harder to achieve as much. As he said, he wouldn't be surprising anyone the second time around. He also knew he would be taking even more abuse than Year One. This meant slashes to the hands and wrist and crosschecks to the back, small things on their own but combined things that had an effect on his body and his patience.

It didn't take long in the new season for a controversy to occur. In a game on October 1, 2004, Sidney was kneed by Frederik Cabana of Halifax, and although Sidney managed to finish the game he missed two weeks because of the injury.

Cabana was given an eight-game suspension for the knee-on-knee hit. This was a punishment that Mooseheads general manager Marcel Patenaude considered too harsh. "I think it is fundamental in the league right now that we have to look at it [the suspension] and make sure that decisions and incidents are evaluated in a fair way." His message was clear: He believed that Cabana received a suspension not because of what he did but because of who he did it to.

...he was without doubt the most important, most-watched hockey player in the world.

If the suspension was a way for the Quebec league to protect its greatest star, it worked. Sidney played the rest of the year without any major injury. Sidney continued to improve and dominate, and because there was a dispute in the NHL which cancelled the season, he was without doubt the most important, most-watched hockey player in the world.

While there might have been some reservation on the part of Hockey Canada to invite the 16-year-old Sidney to the 2004 World Junior Championship, there was never any doubt that he would be counted on to be a leader with the team a year later when the tournament was held in Grand Forks, North Dakota.

He arrived at the final training camp for the 2005 World Junior tournament on December 13, 2004, with exactly that attitude.

"I've learned a lot [since last year]," he said. "I think I'm a better all-round player. I think I'm stronger and faster. I think after experiencing this tournament last year and finishing up in the Q and another half season this year, I have picked up things, like being more consistent defensively."

Team Canada teammate Stephen Dixon played against Sidney all the time in the "Q" (the name everyone called the Quebec league). He played for Cape Breton, and he knew all about what Sidney could do. "He dominated [the league] last year," Stephen said, "but this year he is even more dominant...the thing I noticed that makes him so difficult to play against is that he never makes the same move twice."

Sidney got the biggest bonus of the Team Canada camp when coach Brent Sutter made a brilliant decision by teaming Sidney with Patrice Bergeron, both on and off the ice. They played on the same line, and they shared the same room. At 19 years of age, Patrice had already played one full NHL season. He also won a gold medal with Team Canada at the World Championship in May 2004, which is an even higher level than the World Juniors. Patrice was currently playing professionally in the American Hockey League with Providence while there was no NHL hockey. "He's a great roommate," Sidney said. "I'm trying to learn a lot, getting to know him and learn his tendencies...he's got a lot of experience and he's a very focused guy...I'm just trying to learn as much as I can."

In the team's two exhibition game victories prior to Christmas, Canada beat Finland 6-0 and Switzerland 5-0. Patrice scored five points and Sidney four in those games. The fact that Sidney played right wing to allow Patrice to play at centre further showed his team commitment. The assistant

Sidney screams for a pass during Canada's impressive 3-1 victory over the Czech Republic at the 2005 WJC.

Sidney chases a puck in the corner as teammate Corey Perry watches from behind the Team Sweden goal.

Sidney holds off Swedish forward Loui Eriksson with one arm while stick-handling with the other as he moves up ice during the 2005 World Junior Championship.

coach, Jim Hulton, realized this right away. "There are a lot of kids who, put in that situation, would say, 'Hey, I'm leading the league in scoring. I'm a centreman…Sid just wants to win and it's all about Team Canada."

The day after Christmas, the World Junior Championship began in earnest and Patrice and Sidney were front and centre again. Canada played Slovakia to open the tournament and by the midway point of the game Canada was leading 4-0. Patrice scored two of those goals and Sidney scored the other two! Canada won easily, 7-3.

"It's pretty easy to play with Sidney," the older Patrice said after his three-point game. "He's just got such great vision and it just makes things easier for his linemates." Almost forgotten was the third member of the line, Corey Perry of the London Knights. He was also one of the best players in the world for his age. Sidney, though, went from being a third-line player in the 2004 tournament to playing on the first line this year. The entire country was counting on him to lead Canada to gold for the first time since 1997.

Game two, another overpowering 8-1 win by Canada, this time over Sweden, guaranteed more praise for Canada's dynamic duo. Sidney scored twice more on the power play, one from a near-impossible angle. Both goals came off passes from Patrice who also added a goal for another three-point game. More important for Sidney, he scored after being given a wicked slash to his forearm that hurt him but did not intimidate him.

"You try not to get too unfocused when something like that happens," he explained. "But when you're not near the puck and a guy does that, you want to be sure you bury a couple [of goals]." Sidney's line had now scored seven of the team's 15 goals in the first two games.

Canada's third game, two nights later, was the easiest of all, a 9-0 shellacking of Germany. Sidney scored twice more again, his third straight two-goal game, and Patrice added two assists in the win. They were the top two scorers in the tournament so far.

The next night, the team whipped the Finns 8-1 to end the round robin part of the tournament with a perfect 4-0-0 record. So impressive was the team that even the opposing coach, Finland's Petri Matikainen, praised the Canadian players: "That's the way the game should be played," he said with a smile after the lopsided loss. At least the Finns prevented Sidney from scoring a goal. The big line was held to two assists by Patrice and a goal from Corey Perry. In the four games, the number-one line had accounted for 22 scoring points to lead the tournament. Team Canada had outscored the opposition by a combined 32-5.

Impressive as that might be, Sidney and the rest of the team knew that the upcoming playoff elimination part of the tournament was different from the round robin. In the round robin, a loss would not have meant a great deal. However, in the playoffs, teams that lost went home, and Canada's opponent in the semi-finals was the Czech Republic. "What we've done is in the past," Sidney said at practice before the big match. "We know if we go out there and play the game, we are putting ourselves in a good spot to win."

Canada's performance against the Czechs was awesome. Although the score was close, 3-1, the team allowed only eleven Czech shots the entire game. Wayne Gretzky watched from the stands and was impressed by the team in general and Sidney in particular. "He's got tremendous hockey sense. He moves the puck well. He sees the ice well. And, obviously, he's got great hands. But what is more important," Wayne continued, "is he has fun when he is playing. It's great to see good players play hard and yet really enjoy it, and you can truly feel he enjoys the game…Sidney has been spectacular."

The win set up a gold medal showdown against Russia, their longtime rivals who beat USA 7-2 in the other semi-finals game. It was the fourth straight gold medal game for Canada at the World Juniors, but they had lost each of the last three. In 2002 and 2003, Canada was beaten by the Russians. In 2004 they lost 4-3 to the USA on a fluke goal in the third period. Sidney played in that game, and he was not prepared to lose again. "We are a little more calm," he explained. "We all realize that's why we came here [to win gold]."

The final game also featured a great matchup—Canada's great sensation Sidney Crosby playing Russia's wonder boy Alexander Ovechkin. Alexander gave Canada extra motivation to win when he mentioned the last time the teams played for gold. "Do you remember Halifax?" he asked, referring to the 2003 Russian win in the finals. "Everybody said that Team Canada would win the championship. We won. We proved that Russian hockey was better then." And what about playing against the sensational Sidney? "I've never seen him play," Alexander said. "I think he's a good player. But I don't play against Crosby. I play against Team Canada. Hockey is a team game."

A team game, indeed. Sidney well knew that aspect of hockey. For fans who thought he was all goals and fancy moves, they should have seen him in the third period of the Czech game. He blocked a shot at a critical time by sliding head first toward the shooter. Sidney may have been held without a goal, but he left his mark nonetheless. "I didn't want the puck to go through," he explained of his bravery. "You lay everything on the line. You don't want the puck to go in, so that's part of it—sacrificing your body. It's part of being a hockey team. The glory—and who scores the goals—that doesn't matter to the guys. It all comes down to winning hockey games, and guys want to do whatever it takes." Take that Alexander Ovechkin!

> ***The gold-medal game was an example of Canadian domination from start to finish.***

Although Sidney recorded just one assist in the final game (in the third period), the team crushed Alexander Ovechkin and his Russian teammates, 6-1. It might well have been the greatest World Junior team ever to represent Canada, perhaps the best junior team of all time. As the final horn sounded to end the game, Sidney whooped it up on the bench.

At the final ceremony, when he bent forward so that IIHF president René Fasel could slip a gold medal around his neck, Sidney was nearly in tears. And as he paraded around the ice with the championship trophy above his head and the gold medal around his neck, he was a proud Canadian. "This is a dream come true," he said in the dressing room after. "It's the best thing I've ever done, the best experience I've ever had. It's something you share with your teammates forever...When you get older and look back, you'll be able to say you played with a lot of great hockey players." And with that, he and his teammates packed their bags and went home.

Sidney shakes hands with his Russian counterpart, Alexander Ovechkin, after Canada's gold medal victory.

THE MISSING SWEATER

CHAPTER SIX

Overjoyed, Sidney celebrates his team's gold medal by singing the national anthem with his teammates.

"He's Mister 'Tout le monde'"

Jacques Lamoureux

The only downside to playing in the World Junior Championship is that players have to say goodbye to each other almost right after the final game. All of Team Canada's players had to return to their junior leagues across Canada. So, Team Canada players and staff took a bus to Winnipeg the night they won gold. They spent the night in Canada before heading to the airport and flying to various cities across the country.

Sidney was the only member of the Rimouski Oceanic to play for Canada in Grand Forks, so the next day he boarded Air Canada flight 288 for Montreal. He then took a connecting flight 8964 bound for Mont Joli, Quebec, where he caught up with his Oceanic teammates to resume play in the Quebec league.

When he finally got home, however, he was shocked to see that his red Team Canada sweater with the hallowed number nine on it was not in his equipment bag! It was missing. "There are no words to describe how disappointing and upsetting the whole thing is," his mother, Trina, said sadly after Sidney phoned to tell her the awful news. "Its only value is sentimental, and that is for Sidney."

When he couldn't find the sweater, he was upset beyond what words could describe.

Sidney may be a tough hockey player. He may be big and strong and play with fierce competitive spirit. But, he was still a 17-year-old who was missing something that was very important to him. When he couldn't find the sweater, he was upset beyond what words could describe. "It's hard to explain what he's feeling," his father, Troy, said. "It's just a sick, sick feeling. No one can understand just how important that jersey is. It can't be replaced."

Sidney is overwhelmed by fans as he arrives at the airport in Quebec after winning gold at the World Junior Championship.

"Definitely, I'm upset," Sidney admitted. "You play in the best series and win, and it's a symbol. It's something you want to keep...I don't know what happened to it. It could have been taken or it could have gotten lost. All I know is, it's gone."

Sidney's agent and friend, Pat Brisson, was more angry than sad. "It was his gold-medal jersey," he said. "It wasn't lost. It was stolen. He knows he put it into his equipment bag."

> He had a feeling the sweater went missing while Sidney's equipment was being handled by the airline company.

The only other person on the flight from Winnipeg to Montreal whom Sidney knew was Blair Mackasey, the head scout for Hockey Canada. Blair was certain he saw Sidney's equipment bag being loaded onto the plane. "It was his Rimouski Oceanic bag," he said. "Maybe somebody saw it, put two and two together, knew it was Crosby's, and took the sweater. It would be pretty easy to reach in and grab something," he concluded. That's exactly why Blair never left anything valuable in his Hockey Canada bags when he travelled.

Denis Hainault, the Team Canada director who was with the players the whole trip, was also upset. He was certain that the players' equipment bags were never out of sight, from the moment the players stepped off the ice with gold medals around their neck to the time they boarded planes for different parts of the country the next day in Winnipeg. He had a feeling the sweater went missing while Sidney's equipment was being handled by the airline company.

"We take great pride in what these players do for their country," Denis said, "and we want them to have it [their sweater]." What made matters worse was that all of the players' other sweaters from the tournament—the white sweaters—were being auctioned on the internet. The profits from sales were going to two charities: the Canadian Hockey Foundation and the tsunami relief for South Asia.

Canada Post employee Jean-Marc Saucier poses at the mailbox where a few days earlier he found Sidney's sweater in the mail in Lachute, Quebec.

> But Hockey Canada officials also realized how important Sidney's sweater was to him.

This tsunami cause was extremely important because just after Christmas, while the players were enjoying hockey in North Dakota, an enormous region in the Far Eastern part of the world was devastated by a massive tidal wave called a tsunami. It killed more than 150,000 people. It also destroyed countless homes and left millions of families in need of aid. People from around the world donated billions of dollars to help the affected countries, and Canada's junior hockey players were doing their part by donating their sweaters to the cause.

But Hockey Canada officials also realized how important Sidney's sweater was to him. They took his white sweater off the auction so they could give it to him, and they promised to donate the money that had been bid on it to the tsunami relief anyway. At that time, Sidney's sweater had reached a bid of more than $20,000, by far the highest for any of the team's equipment.

Sidney continued to play for Rimouski, but inside he was upset by the loss of his sweater. Deep down, he hoped that news reports being shown across Canada would lead to its discovery. Just a few days later, he went from sad to happy when the Montreal Police Department contacted him and said they believed they had found the red, number nine sweater.

Just to be sure, Hockey Canada officials confirmed it was the real sweater based on secret security features that were part of the design. Sidney was ecstatic, of course, and believed it was his sweater because, "they said it smells pretty bad, so that's a good sign." Everyone who plays hockey knows the smell of game-worn equipment is not exactly like a bed of roses! Soon enough, the whole story was revealed. Here's what happened.

Jacques Lamoureux was a baggage handler with Air Canada at the Pierre Elliot Trudeau airport in Montreal. Toward the end of his shift one afternoon, he was pushing a luggage cart through the airport terminal. He was transferring luggage from a plane that had arrived in Montreal from Winnipeg to another plane going on to Mont Joli, Quebec. Mr. Lamoureux saw a Rimouski hockey bag on this cart. It was partially open, and just inside he could see a bit of red sweater. He was thinking how much his 14-year-old, hockey-playing daughter would love it. He pulled it out of the bag and stuck it inside his jacket. Just a few minutes later he went home.

"As a single parent, you can't always buy everything they [kids] ask for," Jacques explained later. "I had just replaced all of her equipment. Pants, gloves, shin- pads. At this age, you have to have good equipment." But even before he showed the sweater to his daughter, he knew he had done something wrong. The only way to fix things was to give the sweater back to Sidney.

One night, Jacques went out with a friend who lived near Gatineau, Quebec. Mr. Lamoureux decided to put the sweater in a bag with a newspaper clipping about the missing sweater. He put the yellow bag in the mailbox, like it was a letter, and the next day the mailman, Jean-Marc Saucier, found it and called Hockey Canada in Calgary. Officials there immediately called police who came to pick it up. "It was obviously his sweater," Jean-Marc said. "It had 'CROSBY' in big letters, and on the other side were all the logos and everything."

> *It was partially open, and just inside he could see a bit of red sweater. He was thinking how much his 14-year-old, hockey-playing daughter would love it. He pulled it out of the bag and stuck it inside his jacket.*

"The first thing I did was smell it," said Raymond Deschamps, another postal worker, who received the bag from Jean-Marc. "I've been involved in minor hockey for twenty years, so I know the smell of a worn jersey."

The next day, Sidney was holding his cherished sweater and he was the happiest boy in the world. Meanwhile, Mr. Lamoureux went to the police and confessed his crime. He was charged with theft and the airline suspended him, but he still felt a deep admiration for Sidney Crosby. "He's Mister 'Tout le monde,'" Jacques smiled. What he meant was that Sidney was just like the guy next door. "He's like everybody. He doesn't look like a superstar. He doesn't act like a superstar. I really enjoyed seeing Sidney Crosby smiling with his jersey on the television [after getting it back], even though it will cost me my job…Maybe I was too much of a fan."

The best part of all was that Sidney's white sweater went back on auction on the internet to raise money for charity. A week later, there had been 59 bids, the winning one being for more than $26,000! All's well that ends well.

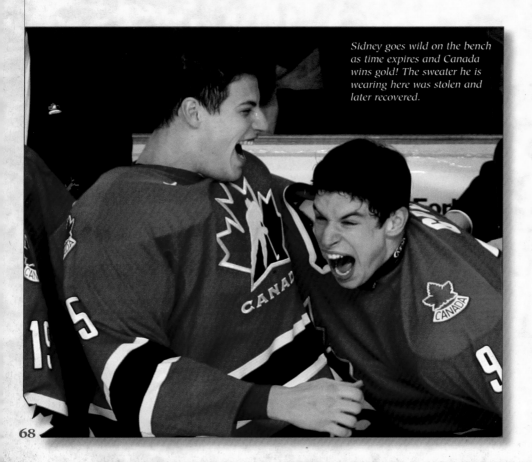

Sidney goes wild on the bench as time expires and Canada wins gold! The sweater he is wearing here was stolen and later recovered.

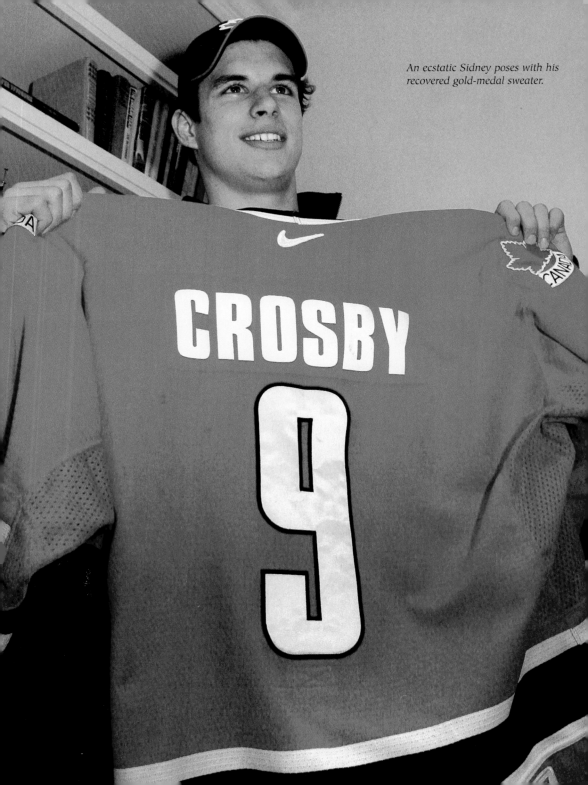

An ecstatic Sidney poses with his recovered gold-medal sweater.

CAPTAIN MARIO WELCOMES THE COLE HARBOUR KID

CHAPTER SEVEN

Sidney celebrates a goal with Rimouski.

"If he wants to stay with us, we have some room."

Mario Lemieux

As luck would have it, the day after Sidney received his recovered Team Canada sweater, his junior team, Rimouski, paid its final visit of the regular season to Halifax, to play the Mooseheads. Because Sidney grew up in nearby Cole Harbour, his family came to see him play—as did the sellout crowd of more than 10,000. Sidney scored two goals, contributed four assists, and led the Oceanic to a big 8-4 victory. He received the loudest cheers of the night, even though he played on the visiting team. Even the Halifax team president, Kevin Cameron, had something nice to say, putting team rivalries aside and calling Sidney "an outstanding Nova Scotian."

> *Sidney was front and centre again, winning five major trophies.*

Sidney finished the 2004-05 season with Rimouski in record-setting fashion. He had 66 goals and 102 assists for a total of 168 points and won the league scoring title by a whopping 54 points over teammate Dany Roussin. The only other two players in QMJHL history to win the scoring title by more than 50 points were Guy Lafleur and Mario Lemieux, both Hall of Fame superstars.

Sidney was also named player of the week the last four weeks of the season and won player of the month each of the last three months. But if anyone thought the personal numbers were more important than the contributions he made to the team, think again. The Oceanic ended the season with a record 28-game unbeaten streak and headed to the playoffs as clear favourites to win the league championship.

On April 6, 2005, during the QMJHL playoffs, the league held its annual Golden Puck Awards dinner. Sidney was front and centre again, winning five major trophies. He won the Michel Brière Trophy as the league's most valuable player, the Offensive Player of the Year Award, the Jean Béliveau Trophy for leading the league in scoring, the Michael Bossy Trophy as the Q's top pro prospect, and the Paul Dumont Trophy as the Personality of the Year.

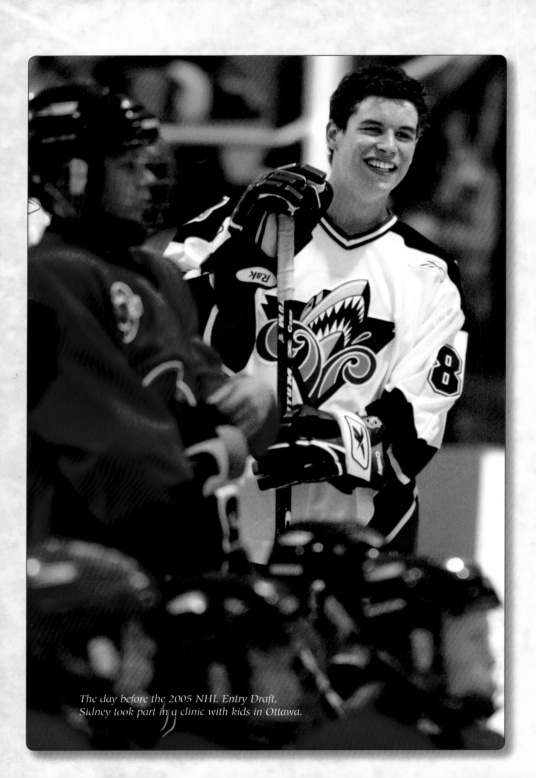

The day before the 2005 NHL Entry Draft,
Sidney took part in a clinic with kids in Ottawa.

A trainer uses calipers to measure Sidney's body fat.

Sidney undergoes fitness testing at the Park Plaza Hotel in Toronto in anticipation of the Entry Draft.

While Sidney was playing to dizzying heights in the QMJHL, the NHL had cancelled the season because the league and players couldn't agree on a new contract. In mid-March, the 2005 Entry Draft scheduled for Ottawa was also cancelled, meaning Sidney would not hear his name called as the first overall choice. "Although I knew this could be a possibility given the current situation," he said, "I feel bad for all of the players who have worked so hard to get to this point."

> "I would not play in a replacement league," he said first off, rejecting the idea of playing with anything less than the best.

Of course, Sidney was asked countless times what his plans were for the fall of 2005 if the NHL had not started up again. "I would not play in a replacement league," he said first off, rejecting the idea of playing with anything less than the best. "The NHL is the NHL for a reason. It's the best league in the world, and with replacement players it would not be. The NHL with real NHL players is where I want to be."

Sidney did say, though, that he would consider playing in Europe starting in the fall of 2005. He could return to Rimouski and rack up amazing statistics for a third consecutive year, but that wouldn't help him develop into the best player he could possibly be. His agent, Pat Brisson, agreed. "He's ready for the next step," Pat said, without trying to insult the QMJHL. If not Europe, Pat suggested, then perhaps the American Hockey League, the league which grooms and develops the NHL's young talents not yet ready for the NHL but too old for junior.

Fortunately, none of these options was needed because in July 2005 the NHL and players agreed to a new deal. However, since there had been no hockey season in over a year, a new method for drafting players had to be used. The league decided that a lottery was the fairest way. "It'll be fun to see how the lottery works out," Sidney said beforehand. Every team had at

Sidney dipsy-doodles with the puck as he crosses centre ice in a QMJHL game.

Sidney is all smiles as his new teammate, Mario Lemieux, welcomes him to Pittsburgh at the 2005 NHL Entry Draft.

least some chance to win the right to draft him, and in the end it was his friend Mario Lemieux in Pittsburgh that came out on top, the same Mario who played with him in the summer, had dinner with him, drove him to the airport. The same Mario who was drafted himself first overall in 1984 when Sidney's dad was drafted! The same Mario who captained Canada to a gold medal at the 2002 Olympics.

"It's a special day for me," Mario said. "Sidney is a great talent. He loves the game of hockey, and he's going to be a great forward in this league. I'm looking forward to playing with him." Then Mario revealed another connection between himself and the Crosbys. In the family basement hangs a photo of Mario scoring on Troy Crosby when they were both playing junior in Quebec. "I was on a breakaway and I roofed it," Mario said with a laugh. "He was a little late on it."

> *"Sidney is a great talent. He loves the game of hockey, and he's going to be a great forward in this league."*

Sidney was happy himself that he could start his career playing with the best. "He's a great role model and to be able to play with him would be something special," the young star said of the Hall of Famer. "We played a few times together on the same line last summer. Playing with Mario [in the NHL] will be pretty special."

Mario then extended the relationship one step further when he invited Sidney to live with him and his family during his first season in Pittsburgh. "If he wants to stay with us," Mario said with a big smile, "we have some room."

After explaining to Tonight Show host Jay Leno that he used to shoot pucks at his family's dryer in the basement, Jay brings out a new dryer for Sidney to show fans across the USA what he did as a kid!

SIDNEY CROSBY BY THE NUMBERS

SIDNEY CROSBY
b. Cole Harbour, Nova Scotia, August 7, 1987
5'10", 185 lbs, shoots left

Selected 1st overall by Rimouski Oceanic at 2003 QMJHL Midget Draft
Selected 1st overall by Pittsburgh Penguins at 2005 NHL Entry Draft

PRE-JUNIOR CAREER		GP	G	A	P	Pim
2001-02	Dartmouth	74	95	98	193	114
2002-03	Shattuck	57	72	90	162	104

QUEBEC MAJOR JUNIOR HOCKEY LEAGUE

Regular Season		GP	G	A	P	Pim
2003-04	Rimouski	59	54	81	135	74
2004-05	Rimouski	62	66	102	168	84

Playoffs		GP	G	A	P	Pim
2004	Rimouski	9	7	9	16	10
2005	Rimouski	13	14	17	31	16

2003-04: CHL Player of the Year; CHL Offensive Player of the Year; CHL Rookie of the Year; CHL First Team All-Star; CHL All-Rookie Team; QMJHL Paul Dumont Trophy (personality of the year); QMJHL Jean Béliveau Trophy (top scorer); QMJHL Michel Bergeron Trophy (offensive rookie of the year); QMJHL RDS Trophy (rookie of the year); QMJHL Michel Brière Trophy (MVP); QMJHL First Team All-Star; QMJHL Rookie All-Star Team

2004-05: CHL Offensive Player of the Year; QMJHL Michel Brière Trophy (MVP); QMJHL Jean Béliveau Trophy (top scorer); QMJHL Michael Bossy Trophy (top pro prospect); QMJHL Paul Dumont Trophy (personality of the year)

INTERNATIONAL		GP	G	A	P	Pim	Finish
2003	CWG	5	9	7	16	16	6th
2003	U-18	5	4	2	6	10	4th
2004	WJC	5	2	4	6	10	Silver
2005	WJC	6	6	3	9	4	Gold

2003: Roland Mitchener Canada Games Award

CWG=Canada Winter Games
U-18=Under-18
WJC=World Junior Championship

ACKNOWLEDGEMENTS

The author would like to thank a number of people who assisted in turning this idea into a book. First, as always, to publisher Jordan Fenn for his continued support. To Bruce Newton and everyone at Hockey Canada for their support of this proposal. To Andre Brin for editing and consulting. To Rob Scanlan and Michael Gray at First Image for their magnificent design. To those who helped with photos, namely Tammy Egan, Andrea Gordon, Nancy Glowinski, Sandor Fizli, Renee Thompson, Craig Campbell and Phil Pritchard at the Hockey Hall of Fame, Szymon Szemberg and Kimmo Leinonen at the IIHF. To my agent, Dean Cooke, and his associates Samantha North and Suzanne Brandreth. And to those near and dear to me for all the other stuff: Mom, Coco, Liz, Ian, Zachary, Emily, Dr. Mary Jane, Jon, Joan, Cathy. Hope to do it again soon.

PHOTO CREDITS

Dave Sandford-Hockey Canada/Hockey Hall of Fame:
p. 4, 36, 39, 42-43, 44, 48, 51, 52-53, 54-55

Matt Manor-Hockey Canada/Hockey Hall of Fame:
p. 6, 8, 10-11, 12, 14, 22

LA Media/Hockey Hall of Fame: p. 17

Tom Dahlin/Hockey Hall of Fame: p. 20, 24-25

Phil MacCallum/Hockey Hall of Fame: p. 31

Rémi Sénéchal/Hockey Hall of Fame: p. 28, 32-33, 34, 35

Shattuck-St. Mary's school: p. 21, 23

Reuters: p. 59, 68, 69, 72, 73 (both), 76, 78, back cover

Dave Sandford/IIHF: p. 60

Canadian Press: p. 47, 62-63, 65, 70, 75

Sandor Fizli: p. 40

Author Photo Back Cover - Mary Jane Nguyen